T0123708

TO WELLNESS AND WINNING FROM WEAKENED AND WEARY

Living beyond grief, loss and illness

DEDORAH S. BROWN

WESTBOW
PRESS®
A DIVISION OF THOMAS NELSON
& ZONDERVAN

WestBow Press books may be ordered through booksellers or by contacting:

WestBow Press
A Division of Thomas Nelson & Zondervan
1663 Liberty Drive
Bloomington, IN 47403
www.westbowpress.com
844-714-3454

ISBN: 978-1-6642-2359-2 (sc)
ISBN: 978-1-6642-2360-8 (hc)
ISBN: 978-1-6642-2358-5 (e)

Library of Congress Control Number: 2021902952

Print information available on the last page.

WestBow Press rev. date: 03/11/2021

This book is dedicated to my parents, my children, my family, my friends, US veterans, and those with hurting hearts en route to healing. I would like to extend special recognition to my husband, Kevin. Thank you for your love, support, prayers, and encouragement throughout the years.

Acknowledgments

I have nothing but love for my maternal side of my family. You keep me uplifted through humor, cooking, singing, dancing, and your competitive spirit during our family game nights.

I am grateful to my paternal side of my family for showing me that I can press on beyond hardships and grief.

I have been nurtured, inspired, and blessed by my church family and its many ministries. Thank you for assisting me through Bible lead lessons as I continue to assist others.

I appreciate my sister circle. You want what's best for me and mine and that matters. You celebrate my successes, and when I am feeling defeated you hold on to me until I am restored, and I love you for that.

My models of servitude are women such as Harriet Tubman, Ida B. Wells, Cicely Tyson, Maya Angelou, Paulette M. Drake, Gladys V. Brown, Frances Ventress, Rachel Mercadel, and Margaret Washington.

I am profoundly grateful to HBCU Dillard University and Tulane University for the education that I received and for the charitable works of the students and alumni.

Lastly, I would like to recognize my father for contributing to my interest and need to express my views and feelings through the ink of a pen.

Introduction

As a child I thought that if I prayed, wished, crossed my fingers, and stayed positive, good things and only good things would happen for me. I believed these things so deeply that when difficulties came my way I had a hard time dealing with what I experienced and an extremely hard time overcoming those misfortunes. In life, tough times will pay you a visit. I still exercise prayer and positive thinking, but I now have an understanding that those beautifully uplifting things will not exclude me or anyone else from having rough days, nor does it mean I disregard what happened. It just makes it easier to deal with. I hope this book gives you a new view and a few words of encouragement when difficulties come your way.

1.

*There is a culture of grief
that must end.*

2.

Your worth is not linked to what someone says to you or how he or she treats you.

3.

When people treat you poorly and you have a hard time being in their presence, remove yourself.

4.

Regulate yourself.

5.

When you are uncomfortable being somewhere, excuse yourself.

6.

*Free yourself from negative
thoughts. Allow joy to come in.*

7.

Find those broken pieces inside of you, validate that they exist and that they deserve some attention, but do not let them dominate your life. Work on getting those pieces repaired.

8.

Give yourself what you have always longed for: love, kindness, and attention.

9.

Many of us are troubled due to past experiences and we find it hard knowing how to conduct ourselves today. Let's get well.

10.

Open yourself to positive possibilities and prosper.

11.

When going through a rough patch, we may latch on to people, places, or things that are not in our best interest, making the problem stay longer than it should and worse than it would have been.

12.

Stop doing things that hinder your healing and well-being.

13.

*Consider what you need to
start and stop in order to have
the life that you deserve.*

14.

You are essential to how you want to live, so get involved.

15.

*If you are connected to things,
people, and places that go against
what makes you whole, retreat.*

16.

When doubt and fear suggest that you can't succeed, think about those you admire who fought for your rights to succeed and the things that they had to overcome.

17.

*Even during your worst days,
take time to reflect on the
good things in your life.*

18.

*Love yourself enough to do
something meaningful with your life.*

19.

Do not let your diagnosis put you in bondage to others.

20.

Make an evacuation plan
from your hardships.

21.

Are you able to be the same person in public that you are in private? If not, why?

22.

Are you responsible for any of the chaos in your life? If so, make better choices.

23.

*People will take you on as a
participant in their endeavors
even when they don't care
about you. Beware!*

24.

Take responsibility for living
your life to the fullest.

25.

There will be seasons when you take care of others, and there will be other seasons when you will be required to take care of yourself and only yourself.

26.

*Seek counsel from those with
good character, not those who
put on good presentations.*

27.

*Renew your spirit and your way
of thinking about yourself.*

28.

If you stop investing in yourself, you will invest in something less rewarding.

29.

Do not work on the blame or the cause. Instead, just work on the healing.

30.

*How long do you plan on turning
over your well-being to someone else?*

31.

People will criticize you for not enduring things that they did not endure and others will criticize you for enduring too much.

32.

Be patient with yourself. You have been through a lot.

33.

It is one thing to make yourself available to assisting others, but when they decide to make a lifestyle out of using your time, home, and funds as a constant source, watch your response.

34.

Do not hide what you should share. Get the help that you need and deserve.

35.

Know when it is not time to take part in other people's issues.

36.

Think about what you want to accomplish and figure out what you must do so that it can emerge.

37.

Forgive yourself for believing that you were all you thought that you could be. Now that you know better, go for the rest of it.

38.

When those who you choose do not choose you, let it be. Poof—be gone!

39.

*Trust in yourself and go
for what you want.*

40.

Conquer your shortcomings.

41.

*People who don't understand
your experience will not
understand your demeanor.*

42.

Your heart may have been previously broken, but your mind does not have to return to that broken place while responding to current experiences. That was that and this is this.

43.

Pay attention to what is being said to you when you are in bad company, then decide how long you plan on staying there.

44.

Address what needs to be addressed.

45.

Yes, you are able to do things.
You are just able to do them
differently than other people.

46.

Do not join a crowd to find yourself.

47.

Love yourself.

48.

*Enjoy being in the presence
of your own being.*

49.

*Protect all of the good things
that make you unique.*

50.

You are responsible for how your life evolves beyond the hurt and pain.

51.

Make time to journal. What comes to mind may startle you, but it can be addressed.

52.

*Love yourself too much to
stay in a bad situation.*

53.

*Face challenges, conquer
them, and move forward.*

54.

*Moving forward can be intimidating,
but if you compare it to where
you are, you may discover that
you better make a move.*

55.

Do not stay in situations where you are miserable for someone else.

56.

Look at your shortcomings to change them, not to bash yourself.

57.

Do not spend time trying not to be yourself. Instead, get in touch with the best version of yourself.

58.

*Learn from those who caused you
pain and try not to inflict those
behaviors on others. Hurt people
do not have to hurt people.*

59.

Do not get in the habit of living badly because when a crisis comes you just may live worse.

60.

You may have deserved certain things but did not get them. You are still here, so it did not take you out, and you are all right.

61.

Even during your bad days, find a reason to smile and commend yourself for sticking in there.

62.

Live past all that has
caused you pain.

63.

Become educated in things that can bring forth positive outcomes for current and future generations.

64.

You can heal from emotional wounds, but you have to commit to the work that it requires.

65.

*Help yourself, contain yourself,
and be conscience of when
you need to deny yourself
in order to save yourself.*

66.

Disrespect does not always come from outside. Sometimes it comes from within. Do not be careless with yourself.

67.

Get well so that you can win.

68.

A great deal of the support that we seek can be found within ourselves.

69.

*Grieving is more difficult
than healing so let's heal.*

70.

You have spent enough years waiting for others to assist you. Do something different by assisting yourself.

71.

Stop hurting yourself so that
you can stop hurting.

72.

Treat yourself to more than just things. Treat yourself with the true desires of your heart.

73.

Stop finding comfort in being the fake version of yourself.

74.

You are worth your time so do not find time to do you— make time to do you!

*There are better things to chase
than mates, fair-weather friends,
and store purchases. Chase healing,
peace, and understanding associated
with who you are, why you are,
and all you are meant to be.*

Printed in the United States
by Baker & Taylor Publisher Services